What's a Million?

By Andra Serlin Abramson

CELEBRATION PRESS
Pearson Learning Group

Contents

Thinking About a Million

You've probably heard the **expression** "He's one in a million." Maybe you've said, "I have a million things to do today." Both of these sayings use the term *million* to express the idea of a large number. Have you ever thought about what a million is or what a million of something looks like?

A Million Ways to Say...

The term *million* has made its way into our language in some surprising ways. Have you heard of all the expressions below? Do you know what each one means?

Thanks a million!

There are a million reasons to...

A one in a million chance...

That's the million-dollar question.

If I've told you once, I've told you a million times...

There are millions of fish in the sea.

About 38 million people in China watched the Chinese team play in the 2002 World Cup Soccer championship on a live Internet broadcast.

A million is a very large number. It is written numerically like this: 1,000,000. The base word *mill* comes from a Latin word for "thousand." In English, a million is much larger than a thousand. It is 1,000 times more than the number 1,000.

You'll notice that the number 1,000,000 is the number one with six zeros after it. In fact, 1,000,000 follows certain rules like every other number.

In July 2005, nearly a million people attended the Live 8 concert in Philadelphia.

For example, you can add to a million. You can also subtract from it, multiply by it, and divide numbers into it. You can have a million of something, but you may need to have some place large to put your collection. You can even hope to earn a million dollars someday. A million is just a number like any other!

While a million is a big number, there are numbers much bigger than a million. A billion is 1,000 times bigger than a million. A **trillion** is 1,000 times bigger than that! You can find out just how big a number is by counting the number of digits.

Writing large numbers takes up a lot of space. So, mathematicians have created a way to make keeping track of all those zeros easier. This shorthand is called "The Power of Ten." Using The Power of Ten, a million would be written like this: 10^6. To **interpret** this symbol, you would read it as "10 to the power of 6." This translates into 1 followed by six zeros, or 1,000,000.

A million is a large number, but there are numbers much, much bigger than that!

Just How Big Can Numbers Get?

Name	Power of Ten	Numerically
Million	10^6	1,000,000
Billion	10^9	1,000,000,000
Trillion	10^{12}	1,000,000,000,000
Quadrillion	10^{15}	1,000,000,000,000,000
Quintillion	10^{18}	1,000,000,000,000,000,000
Septillion	10^{24}	1,000,000,000,000,000,000,000,000
Decillion	10^{33}	1,000,000,000,000,000,000,000,000,000,000,000

Start Counting

Ready…set…start counting to a million! You probably wouldn't get very far in this exercise before you realized how time-consuming it would be. If you were counting at a rate of one number each second, it would still take you more than eleven and a half days to count to a million. That's if you never took a break!

You would fall asleep long before you could count to a million.

A nanometer is a tiny unit of measurement that equals one-billionth of a meter. The head of this pin is about one million nanometers from end to end.

A million is such a big number that you may be wondering how often it is used. The answer is that there are certain things that can most easily be counted in millions. The number of tons of apples Americans eat every year is counted in millions. The letters mailed every day in the United States number in the millions.

More than 100 million Americans used the Internet each month from October 2000 to October 2001.

The daily mail volume in the United States averaged 670 million pieces in 2003.

In the United States, there were more than fifty metropolitan areas with populations over 1 million people in 2005.

Our country's **population** is also measured in millions. The U.S. government uses a **census** to count every American. According to this counting **method**, there were almost 300 million (300,000,000) U.S. citizens in 2005!

Some of the largest cities in the United States have more than a million people living in them. More than 8 million people live in New York City. The next highest population is in Los Angeles, with more than 3 million people.

The population of the entire Earth is measured in billions, not millions. The countries of China and India each had more than a billion **residents** in 2005. The U.S. Census Bureau believes that by the year 2045 there will be more than 9 billion people living on Earth.

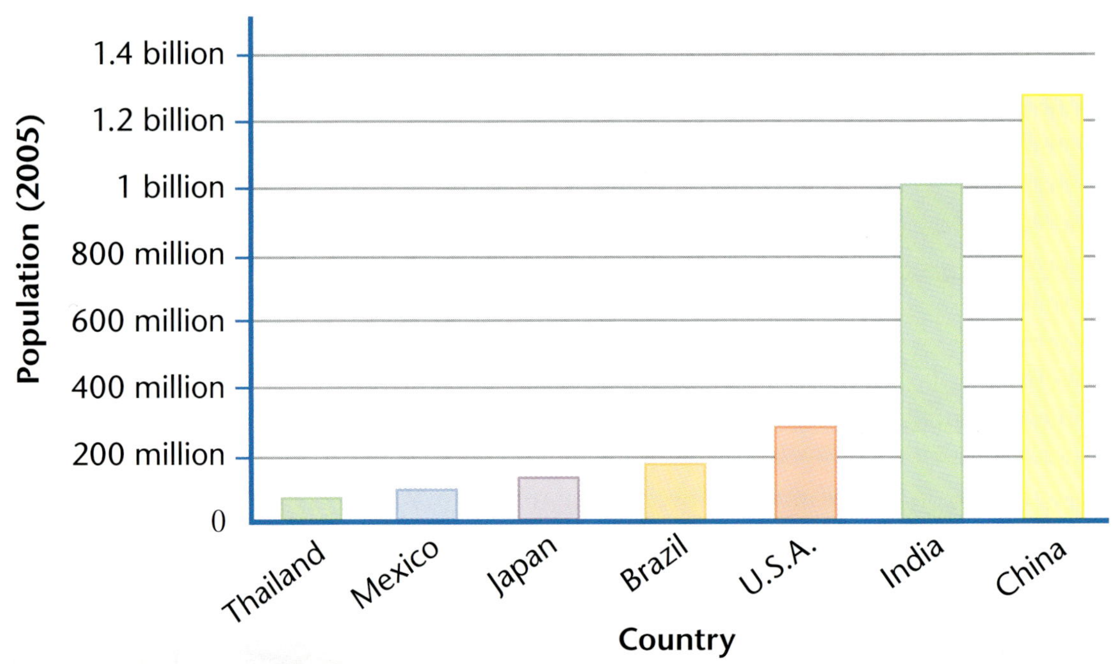

Population of Selected Countries Around the World

China has the largest population of any country in the world.

It will take the average American
worker more than twenty-seven years
to earn the million dollars shown here.

If You Had a Million Dollars

Imagine you had a million dollars. What would you buy? Spending a million dollars is fun to think about. Do you know how much you'd get for your money? Could you buy an airplane? Would you be able to get every video game you've ever wanted?

The answer might depend on some things you've never considered. This is because the value of money doesn't stay the same. It changes depending on **circumstances**. For example, the same house that costs a million dollars in California perhaps could be bought for half of that in Nebraska. In this case, location is the reason for the difference.

What year it is may also affect how much your million would buy. For instance, houses built fifty years ago may have increased dramatically in value, or price. This is known as **appreciation**.

Appreciation means that the value or price of something goes up over time. In fact, the house in Nebraska may someday be worth a million dollars. By then, the value of the house in California may have increased to 2 million dollars.

The country you live in also determines what a million dollars will buy. You probably know that different countries use different currencies, or money. The United States uses dollars. China uses the yuan. Mexico uses the peso. While a million U.S. dollars is considered a lot of money, a million pesos will not buy as much. In fact, it's worth less than one-tenth of a million dollars, or less than $100,000.

This 100-peso note is worth about $9.27 in American dollars.

A person who has more than a million dollars is called a millionaire. Now that you know a little bit more about the value of money, what would you buy if you were a millionaire?

Perhaps you'd like to collect rare objects, such as old coins, stamps, or cars. You could buy great works of art. You might buy yourself a private jet. It's fun to imagine the possibilities.

Valuable objects such as these can sell for a million dollars or more.

This very light jet costs around $1,200,000.

This 1918 "Inverted Jenny" stamp block sold for $2,970,000.

This 1932 Duesenberg Model J Car is worth $1,001,000.

Time Flies!

How old are you? Is that more than a million minutes? Is it more than a million hours? If you are reading this book, chances are you're a lot older than a million minutes. You had already reached that point by the time you were two years old.

To figure out about how many millions of minutes you've lived, try this calculation:

- Multiply your age × 365 (the number of days in a year).

- Multiply this answer by 24 (the number of hours in a day).
- Finally, multiply that number by 60 (the number of minutes in an hour).

By the time you are ten, you have spent nearly 1,800,000 minutes, 30,000 hours, or 1,250 days, sleeping.

If you are ten years old, your method of calculating your age would look like this:

10 x 365 x 24 x 60 = 5,256,000 minutes.

You would have to live a long time to live a million hours, though. You would not reach that number until you were more than 114 years old!

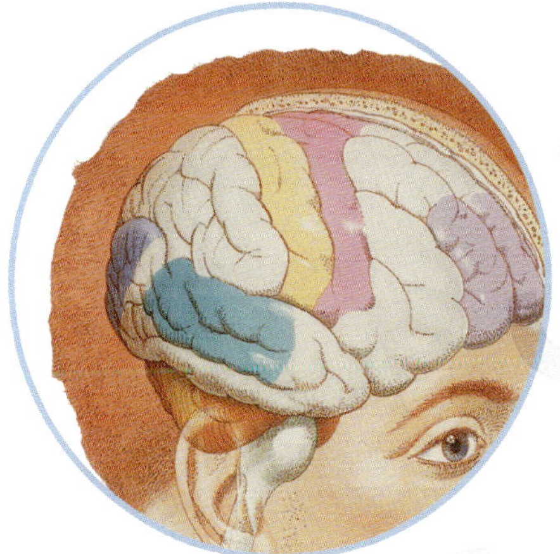

Each person is born with more than 100 billion brain cells.

Recent record holders for the title "World's Oldest Person" have lived to be 115 and 116 years old.

Now, think about what it may have been like on Earth a million years ago. Do you picture houses and streets and stores like the ones we have now? Do you think there would be dinosaurs roaming the Earth? Actually, the answer is somewhere in between.

According to fossil records, dinosaurs had already disappeared from the Earth 65 million (65,000,000) years ago. A million years ago, there were no houses or streets.

Fossil records show that the dinosaurs roamed Earth for about 185 million years.

There were many plants and animals that
you would recognize on Earth a million years
ago. There were also huge animals, such as
mammoths and saber-toothed cats, that no longer
live today. They lived during the last Ice Age,
when much of the Earth was covered with ice.

The largest saber-toothed cat
was about the size of a lion but
was much heavier, weighing
in at about 440 pounds.

There are some things you may be able to see and touch that are more than a million years old. Can you guess what might be **durable** enough to last that long? If you thought of rocks, you'd be right. Your local natural history museum might have some of these million-year-old wonders for you to see.

Just take a walk outside and look around. It could be that rock you find is more than a million years old.

Amber

Trilobite

Your local museum of natural history may have rocks, fossils, gems, and other materials that are more than a million years old.

Millions of years ago, some trees died in Arizona and were buried. They gradually petrified, and the wood became like stone.

Omega Centauri, the largest ball of stars in our galaxy, has about 10 million stars orbiting its center.

Far and Away

Look out into space sometime at night. You may see the Moon, stars, and planets. Have you ever thought about how far away these objects are from Earth?

The Sun is the closest star to Earth. Earth rotates around the Sun at a distance of about 93,000,000 miles. That is so far that it takes the light from the Sun more than eight minutes just to reach Earth.

Now, imagine you were going to travel to the Sun. You know that the Sun is too hot to get close to. People would have a hard time traveling to the Sun even if it were not so hot. What's more, traveling even one million miles takes a long time. A million miles would take you around the **circumference** of Earth about forty times.

Traveling at 550 miles per hour, the cruising speed of a typical jet plane, it would take you more than 1,818 hours to go a million miles. That's almost seventy-six days—even if you never stopped to refuel or to take a break.

The circumference of Earth was first reliably measured by Greek mathematician Eratosthenes more than 2,000 years ago.

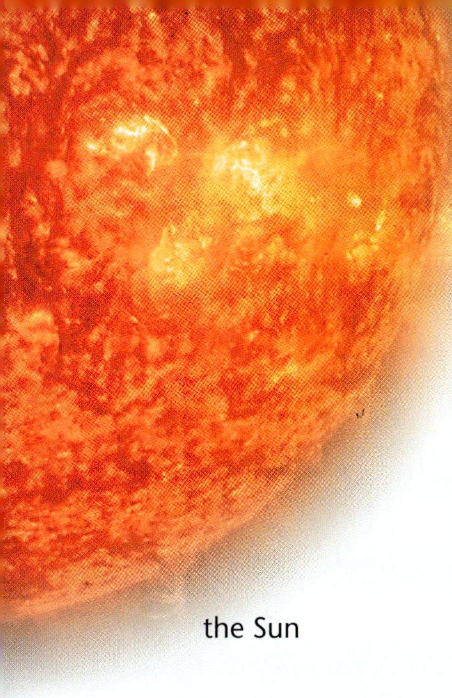

the Sun

Now, what if you had to travel 93,000,000 miles? Even if you could go ten times faster than the jet plane, it would still take you almost two years of constant traveling just to get to the Sun.

Engineers are always trying to figure out how to make aircraft that are more durable and fly faster. So, maybe it won't be long before a million miles in space travel becomes just like a trip around the circumference of Earth.

This machine, called the Z machine, created the hottest temperature ever on Earth, about 3.6 billion degrees Fahrenheit. This is hotter than the interior of the Sun.

Thanks a Million!

While a million is a large number, it is an important and useful number to know. Whether counting population or distance, time or money, you'll be able to think more clearly about large numbers once you understand their **properties** and value. Once you know all about a million, you'll probably find that there are a million and one uses for your information!

If you were to count all the grains of sand in a beach pail, there would be many millions of them.

Glossary

appreciation	a rise in value or price, especially over time
census	an official count of the people of a or area country
circumference	the size of something round as measured by the distance around it
circumstances	the existing conditions or facts
durable	able to last over a long period of time; able to stand wear and tear
expression	a group of words that together create a phrase; a saying
interpret	to explain the meaning of
method	a way of doing something
population	the number of inhabitants living in a particular place
properties	features or qualities of something
residents	people living in a place
trillion	large number that represents 1,000,000,000,000

Index